LGBTQ+ DISCRIMINATION

Rachael Morlock

NEW YORK

Published in 2021 by The Rosen Publishing Group, Inc.
29 East 21st Street, New York, NY 10010

Copyright © 2021 by The Rosen Publishing Group, Inc.

All rights reserved. No part of this book may be reproduced in any form without permission in writing from the publisher, except by a reviewer.

First Edition

Editor: Theresa Emminizer
Designer: Michael Flynn
Interior Layout: Rachel Rising

Photo Credits: Cover, p.1 cofotoisme/iStock/Getty Images; cover Cosmic_Design/Shutterstock.com; cover, pp. 6, 8, 10, 12, 14, 18, 20, 22, 24, 26, 30, 32, 36, 38, 40 Vitya_M/Shutterstock.com; cover Ekaphon maneechot/Shutterstock.com; pp. 3, 5 Tirachard Kumtanom/Shutterstock.com; pp. 3, 17 ABO PHOTOGRAPHY/Shutterstock.com; pp. 3, 29 Beatriz Vera/Shutterstock.com; pp. 3,35 Monkey Business Images/Shutterstock.com; pp. 3, 43 Ink Drop/Shutterstock.com; p. 6 Prostock-studio/Shutterstock.com; p. 7 Sata Production/Shutterstock.com; p. 8 Serhii Bobyk/Shutterstock.com; p. 9 Borislav Bajkic/Shutterstock.com; p. 10 Peter Hermes Furian/Shutterstock.com; pp. 11, 25 Rawpixel.com/Shutterstock.com; p. 12 Aohodesign/Shutterstock.com; p. 13 Sandra van der Steen/Shutterstock.com; p. 15 Sam Wordley/Shutterstock.com; p. 18 Richard Bailey/Corbis/Getty Images; p. 19 chip art/Shutterstock.com; p. 20 weniliou/Shutterstock.com; p. 21 nito/Shutterstock.com; p. 23 SAUL LOEB/Contributor/AFP/Getty Images; p. 24 Kanok Sulaiman/Shutterstock.com; p. 26 Africa Studio/Shutterstock.com; p. 27 fizkes/Shutterstock.com; p. 31 wera Rodsawang/Moment/Getty Images; p. 33 RimDream/Shutterstock.com; p. 37 Elena Elisseeva/Shutterstock.com; p. 38 Motortion Films/Shutterstock.com; p. 39 FatCamera/E+/Getty Images; p. 40 tanuha2001/Shutterstock.com; p. 41 Brocreative/Shutterstock.com; p.42 Sunflowerr/Shutterstock.com; p. 45 Olesia Bilkei/Shutterstock.com.

Some of the images in this book illustrate individuals who are models. The depictions do not imply actual situations or events.

Library of Congress Cataloging-in-Publication Data

Names: Morlock, Rachael, author.
Title: LGBTQ+ discrimination / Rachael Morlock.
Description: New York : Rosen Publishing, [2021] | Series: @RosenTeenTalk |
   Includes index.
Identifiers: LCCN 2020006039 | ISBN 9781499468168 (library binding) | ISBN
   9781499468151 (paperback)
Subjects: LCSH: Homophobia—Juvenile literature. | Transphobia—Juvenile
   literature. | Sexual minorities—Juvenile literature. |
   Discrimination—Juvenile literature.
Classification: LCC HQ76.4 .M67 2021 | DDC 306.76/6—dc23
LC record available at https://lccn.loc.gov/2020006039

Manufactured in the United States of America

CPSIA Compliance Information: Batch #BSR20. For further information contact Rosen Publishing, New York, New York at 1-800-237-9932.

CONTENTS

WHAT DOES LGBTQ+ MEAN? 4

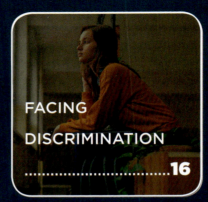
FACING DISCRIMINATION 16

SERIOUS EFFECTS 28

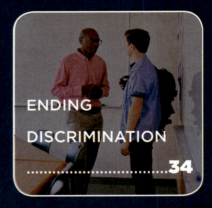
ENDING DISCRIMINATION 34

SHOW YOUR PRIDE! 42

GLOSSARY 46

INDEX 48

Chapter 1

What Does LGBTQ+ Mean?

I think I've always known I was gay. I had my first crush on a boy when I was in first grade. My uncle's gay, so I felt pretty safe coming out to my family. It was harder telling my friends. Some kids at school still make gay jokes when I'm around.

I met Sam this summer when he joined the swim team. We really like each other. I want to tell our friends we're dating, but Sam's not sure. No one else knows he's gay. He's afraid of what might happen. At his last school, a boy was beaten up for being gay. To be honest, I'm nervous too. Everyone knows about me, but they've never seen me with a boyfriend.

EVERYONE IS DIFFERENT

Every person has an individual identity. Identity is shaped by a person's **experiences**, hopes, and skills. Sexuality and **gender** are part of identity too.

> Everyone's sexual identity should be accepted. It's part of who they are, just like their hair, eye, or skin color.

LGBTQ+ is a group of sexual and gender identities. It stands for lesbian, gay, bisexual, transgender, and queer. The plus sign shows that there are even more groups besides these.

Sadly, many LGBTQ+ people are treated unfairly. Everyone should have the right to be who they are and love whom they love. It's important to respect and accept LGBTQ+ people.

Fact!
All sexual identities are normal. They aren't chosen. They're a natural part of every person.

MAJORITIES AND MINORITIES

The majority of people are heterosexual and cisgender. Heterosexual means that they're attracted to, or drawn to, members of the opposite sex. Cisgender means that their gender identity matches the one marked down for them at birth. People who are not heterosexual or cisgender are often called LGBTQ+. This group is a **minority**. But they matter just as much as the majority.

SEX AND GENDER

When a baby is born, it's assigned, or given, a sex. Doctors look at a baby's body parts. They usually decide if it's male or female. Not all bodies fit into these groups, though. Some are intersex. They're born with mixed male and female parts.

The sex of a baby can be seen even before birth.

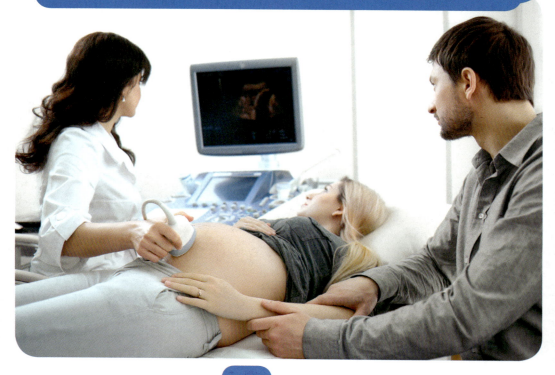

People often have firm ideas about males and females. They expect them to behave, or act, in certain ways. Social ideas about how the sexes should behave are called gender. But sex and gender are more than just your body parts. Your inner identity matters too.

Fact!
Intersex babies are often given operations to make their body parts fit a standard sex. These are usually not needed. They can be harmful to **mental** and **physical** health.

INNER IDENTITY

Your inner identity might not match the sex and gender you were assigned at birth. Most people have a strong sense of who they are. That could be male, female, a mix of the two, or neither one.

WHOM DO YOU LIKE?

Sexual orientation is an important part of identity too. It tells you what kind of person you're attracted to. Your sexual orientation usually becomes clear as you get older. You might become aware of it as your body changes. It can also change over time. Sexual orientations include asexual, bisexual, gay, lesbian, pansexual, queer, and straight.

In the United States, 4.5 percent of adults **identify** themselves as lesbian, gay, bisexual, or transgender.

ABCs of Sexual Orientation

Asexual: Someone who is not sexually attracted to others.

Bisexual: Someone who is attracted to both men and women.

Gay: Someone who is attracted to members of the same sex. Gay men are attracted to men. Gay women are attracted to women.

Lesbian: A gay woman. Lesbians are sexually attracted to other women.

Pansexual: A person who is attracted to individuals. Sexuality and gender are not important factors.

Queer: A term that includes all minority sexual and gender identities.

Straight: A person who is attracted to the opposite sex. Straight men are attracted to women. Straight women are attracted to men. This is also called heterosexual.

BEING TRANSGENDER

Transgender is not a sexual orientation. A transgender person can have any orientation. Being transgender is only tied to gender.

For transgender people, their gender identity doesn't match the one assigned at birth. For example, a person could be raised as a girl but identify as a boy. A transgender person may choose to share their real identity. They might change their gender expression. This refers to things like hair, clothing, and body parts. They offer clues about gender identity.

TRANSGENDER TRANSITIONS

Changing gender expression from male to female or female to male is called transitioning. There are no requirements for transitioning. It's different for every transgender person. They may choose any of the following ways to transition:

- Tell friends, family, and others about their gender identity.
- Use a name that matches their gender identity.
- Ask others to use correct pronouns for them. A trans woman may wish for people to use "she" and "her" when talking about her. A trans man may wish for people to use "he" and "him." Others may prefer "they" or "them."
- Make hair, clothing, and gender expression choices that feel right for their gender identity.

- Take male or female **hormones**. These can change the way they look and feel.
- Seek operations that change their body to match their true gender.

Transitioning is not easy. You can support, or help, people who are transitioning by always using their chosen name and pronouns.

OTHER GENDER EXPRESSIONS

Not all people identify as male or female. Some people are genderqueer or gender nonbinary. That means that their identity falls between or outside of male and female genders.

Chapter 2

Facing Discrimination

The worst thing about being a lesbian is keeping it a secret. Sometimes I feel like no one really knows me. But I just don't feel safe coming out.

Kids at school say rude things about lesbians. I feel so bad when I read mean comments on social media about sexuality. I've even heard my parents putting down LGBTQ+ people. What if they kick me out when I tell them?

I'll be applying to college soon. In some ways, I can't wait to try out my real identity somewhere new. At the same time, I'm worried I won't get in. What if the schools find out I'm gay? I don't want to be judged for just one part of who I am.

> Keeping your sexual identity a secret can make you feel very lonely.

PROTECTING MINORITIES

Discrimination is treating others unfairly because of their identity. LGBTQ+ people face discrimination every day. They face discrimination for whom they love. They face discrimination for how they express their gender. And they face discrimination for the way their bodies look.

About 92 percent of LGBTQ+ teens hear **negative** messages about being LGBTQ+ on the internet, in school, and among peers.

LGBTQ+ people are minorities. That means their rights need to be protected, or kept safe. They have the same basic human rights as heterosexual and cisgender people. LGBTQ+ people should not be treated differently because of their sexual identity.

Fact!

Sometimes discrimination is legal, or lawful. Laws can make life hard for LGBTQ+ people. Discrimination can also be social. This is when LGBTQ+ people are hurt or left out by others.

WHY DO PEOPLE DISCRIMINATE?

Many people believe that all males and all females should behave, look, and love in certain ways. LGBTQ+ people act against these ideas. That makes some people angry and afraid. Fear of LGBTQ+ people is called homophobia. It's often made worse by religions that say it's wrong to be LGBTQ+.

AROUND THE WORLD

Much work is needed to make the world safe for everyone. Not all governments protect LGBTQ+ people. Instead, many **punish** them. Same-sex relationships are against the law in 72 countries.

Same-sex marriage became legal in Taiwan in 2019. Taiwan is the first country in Asia to take this step.

Being LGBTQ+ is legal other places. But there's still discrimination. Often, LGBTQ+ people are unfairly blocked from services. These include housing, education, jobs, and health care.

Violence happens everywhere. People who are or are thought to be LGBTQ+ are often harassed. That could mean being called names, beaten up, or killed.

Fact!

LGBTQ+ people can be arrested and punished in one-third of the world. Some can be jailed for life. In a few countries, an LGBTQ+ person can be put to death because of whom they love.

EQUAL RIGHTS

Some countries actively guard LGBTQ+ rights. For example, same-sex couples can marry in 28 countries. Other countries are making it easier for transgender people. They can officially change their identity. There's still a long way to go to make sure that LGBTQ+ people have equal rights.

IN THE UNITED STATES

Having a same-sex relationship was against the law for a long time in the United States. Today, LGBTQ+ relationships and marriage are legal across the country. However, many states still allow discrimination in housing, employment, and public places. Only 20 states offer legal protection in all three areas.

LGBTQ+ people sometimes experience discrimination when:
- Applying for a job
- Being considered for a raise or new position
- Applying to schools
- Buying or renting a home
- Adopting children
- Voting
- Seeking health care

More than half of all LGBTQ+ adults in the United States have experienced **threats**, hurtful names and comments, sexual harassment, and violence from individuals.

IN SCHOOLS

Schools should be safe places. That's not the case for many LGBTQ+ kids. Most LGBTQ+ students say they've been bullied by peers. Some school rules also discriminate against LGBTQ+ students.

All students have a right to go to school without discrimination. In most cases, state or federal laws protect your rights. Seek out a trusted adult if you are LGBTQ+ and need support. This could be a teacher, school **counselor**, librarian, school nurse, or coach.

Transgender students risk being "outed" by teachers if their correct name and pronouns aren't used. Dress codes can be a problem. So can rules about clubs and sports teams.

FACING DISCRIMINATION

LGBTQ+ students face daily discrimination in school. In 2017:

- 87 percent were bullied because of their gender or sexual identity.

- 57 percent were sexually harassed. This includes unwanted touching or sexual comments.

- 34 percent stayed home from school at least one day in a month because they felt unsafe.

For transgender students in school:

- 42 percent weren't allowed to use their chosen name and pronouns.

- 46 percent were required to use the wrong bathroom.

- 43 percent were required to use the wrong locker room.

DISCRIMINATION ONLINE

Over 48 percent of LGBTQ+ students have been bullied online. This is cyberbullying. It usually takes place through texts or social media. That might mean that harmful photos of a person are passed around. Spreading private stories or information is cyberbullying. So is calling names and sending threats.

Many cyberbullying attacks are anonymous, meaning the bully's identity is unknown. Also, most teens are highly connected online. They may feel like there's no escape. If you see cyberbullying, report it. Tell a trusted adult or notify the online service in use.

Find Help!

If you can, reach out to your friends, family, or school for support if you're being bullied. You can also check out these **resources**:

It Gets Better Project
itgetsbetter.org
Share your story, or hear from others who are struggling with LGBTQ+ discrimination.

LGBT National Youth Talkline
800-246-7743
www.glbthotline.org/youth-talkline.html
This free resource gives young people an opportunity to talk without being judged. The call center is staffed by members of the LGBTQ+ community.

Most LGBTQ+ students spend more time online than their peers. The internet can be important for connection, support, and information. It needs to be safe.

Chapter 3

Serious Effects

My friend Lilly asked me to go to a new club with her after school. Lilly's great, but I don't want to go. Meeting new people really wears me out. All I want lately is to be alone.

Everything feels off. Being transgender can be so hard. Sometimes I don't know where I belong. Which bathroom is it okay for me to use? Which sports team can I play on? How many times do I have to remind people about my pronouns? It feels like there's never room for me no matter where I go.

Sometimes I think it will be easier when I'm older. There are other days when I just don't know. Will it ever get better?

> Being different can be hard. But you are not alone!

DISCRIMINATION IS DANGEROUS

Discrimination can be very harmful. It can result in joblessness and homelessness. Many LGBTQ+ people are turned away by doctors and counselors. School discrimination can lead to poor grades or thoughts of dropping out.

Just being part of a minority group causes **stress**. LGBTQ+ people are often afraid of being discriminated against. This can keep them from seeking the services they need. In an emergency, 15 percent of LGBTQ+ people avoided calling the police. Another 18 percent did not seek health care.

> Negative attitudes mean that some LGBTQ+ people are **rejected** by their families. Young LGBTQ+ people are more likely to experience homelessness. Up to 40 percent of homeless youth are LGBTQ+.

MENTAL HEALTH

Feeling rejected is harmful to mental health. The stress caused by discrimination can build up. Many LGBTQ+ people experience depression as a result. Depression is a sad mood that lasts a long time. It gets in the way of living your life. Depressed teens may turn to unhealthy habits to deal with their stress.

Compared to their peers, young LGBTQ+ people are:

- Twice as likely to use drugs and alcohol
- More than twice as likely to purposely hurt themselves, or self-harm
- More than twice as likely to think about suicide, or killing themselves
- Four times as likely to attempt suicide
- Transgender teens are four times more likely to experience depression

Find Help!

No matter how alone you feel, things can get better. LGBTQ+ people and allies are ready to support you. They can help when you're feeling **confused** or upset. If you're thinking about hurting yourself or you need to talk, call:

The Trevor Project
866-488-7386

Trans Lifeline
877-565-8860

The National Suicide Prevention Line
800-273-8255

These hotlines are free and confidential. That means they won't share your information with anyone else.

Chapter 4

Ending Discrimination

The writing on the bathroom door shocked me. My stomach did a flip when I read it. All I could think was that I hoped no one else had seen it yet. Luckily Mr. Parker was right around the corner. When I told him about it, he called a custodian to have it cleaned off.

I just keep thinking about that horrible message. I know there are some gay kids in school. I'd like to make it clear that I'm here for them. Whoever wrote that message does not speak for me.

There must be something I can do. I want to show LGBTQ+ people that I support them. They deserve to feel safe and welcome at school just like me.

> Fighting against discrimination is everyone's job. If you see something hurtful, say something about it!

HOW TO BE AN ALLY

An ally is a heterosexual or cisgender person who supports LGBTQ+ people. Being an ally means taking action.

- Always use an LGBTQ+ person's preferred name and pronouns.
- Think before you speak. Never use slurs or call someone names. A slur is a put-down. Saying "that's so gay" is a slur.
- Listen first.
- Let others know that anti-LGBTQ+ jokes are not funny.
- Don't assume that everyone is straight.
- Take part in events that support LGBTQ+ people. Look for Day of Silence, National Coming Out Day, No Name-Calling Week, Transgender Day of Remembrance, and Ally Week.

- Work to change harmful school rules.
- Learn about your **privilege**. What challenges do LGBTQ+ students face that you don't notice?
- Notice your own **prejudices**. Work to change them.
- Speak up when you see bullying in person or online.
- Treat everyone with respect.

> You might make mistakes as you're learning to be an ally. Just keep an open mind. Don't be afraid to say sorry if you've done something hurtful.

CONNECT!

Find more ideas through GLSEN (the Gay, Lesbian, and Straight Education Network). The organization focuses on LGBTQ+ movements led by students. Visit **www.glsen.org**.

STARTING A GSA

Anyone can make their school safer for LGBTQ+ students. One way is to join or start a GSA. This stands for Gay-Straight Alliance or Gender and Sexuality Alliance. GSAs have two purposes. They form spaces where students of all sexual and gender identities can come together in support. They also push for change. They aim to end discrimination for LGBTQ+ students in their schools and larger communities. GSAs improve schools. They make them more welcoming and accepting for LGBTQ+ students.

Being part of a GSA can help LGBTQ+ students be healthier and safer. Having support makes a big difference.

How to Start a GSA

1) Look into your school's rules for starting a club.

2) Find an advisor. Look for a staff member who has shown support for LGBTQ+ students before.

3) Meet with an **administrator**. Talk about how GSAs make schools stronger.

4) Find a private meeting place.

5) Announce your first meeting. Make signs. Invite your friends. Plan snacks!

6) At your meeting, come up with rules to keep everyone safe.

7) Start planning how to change your school, community, and the world!

STAY SAFE ONLINE

LGBTQ+ people are at higher risk of online discrimination. But the internet is still a necessary tool. It can help teens find support, connect with other LGBTQ+ people, be themselves, and share their identity. Some simple steps can help protect against online harassment.

Online Guidelines:
- Be aware of your privacy settings on social media. You can decide who sees what you post.
- Always be careful about sharing private information or photographs. Be wary if strangers you meet online ask for them.
- Report negative and harmful messages to the online service you're using.

- Block or unfollow people who make you feel bad about yourself.
- Follow positive accounts and hashtags, like #LoveIsLove, #TransIsBeautiful, and #YouMatter.
- Be polite and respectful.
- If the internet is giving you stress, take a break. It's okay to unplug for awhile.

Connect!

Check out these safe LGBTQ+ chat spaces to connect with your peers, find information, and get support:

Q Chat Space
https://www.qchatspace.org/

Gender Spectrum Lounge
https://genderspectrum.org/lounge/

The internet is an important form of connection for LGBTQ+ teens. About 73 percent of LGBTQ+ teens say they are more honest about themselves online.

Chapter 5

SHOW YOUR PRIDE!

Being a young LGBTQ+ person can be hard in many ways. It can also be positive and fun. Your sexual and gender identity is an important part of you. Identifying as LGBTQ+ can connect you with a large and welcoming community. Here you will find people who support, understand, and value you. Honor this part of your identity. When you join together with other LGBTQ+ people, you make the community stronger. Being yourself is your best gift to the world.

FROM PREJUDICE TO PRIDE

Pride month provides fun and colorful ways for LGBTQ+ people and allies to come together. It's rooted in the 1969 Stonewall **riots** in New York City. This was an attack on the LGBTQ+ community. After the riots, many people became more open about their sexuality. They worked for greater rights.

Pride month happens every June. It's observed with parades around the United States and the world. The first Pride parade took place in 1970. It marked one year since the Stonewall riots.

The rainbow flag has been a sign of LGBTQ+ pride since 1978. It was first made by Gilbert Baker for the San Francisco Pride event.

Better Every Day

Sam and I just went to our first school dance as a couple. I can't say we weren't nervous. Both of us were sweating as we headed into the gym holding hands. But then Mrs. Parker smiled at us, and it felt like we were safe. Soon some of my friends from GSA were all around us. They wanted to know everything about how we got together. Sam laughed and blushed. I was so proud to be there with him.

I know there might still be trouble. But tonight felt like a giant high-five. Whatever is ahead, Sam and I can handle it. We have my parents, our GSA, and friends to help us. I know things will just keep getting better.

GLOSSARY

administrator: Someone whose job is to run a school or company.
confused: Feeling unsure or unable to think clearly.
counselor: Someone who talks with people about their feelings and problems and who gives advice.
experience: Skill or knowledge you get by doing or seeing something.
gender: The behaviors linked to the different sexes in society.
hormone: A natural substance produced in the body that controls the way the body develops.
identify: To tell what something or someone is.
mental: Related to the mind.
minority: A group of people who are different in some way from the larger part of a population.
negative: Not positive or helpful.
physical: Related to the body.
prejudice: An unfair feeling of dislike for a person or group because of race, religious or political beliefs, or sexual or gender identity.

privilege: Special advantages because of who you are.

punish: To cause someone pain or loss for an act they committed.

reject: To refuse or turn away.

resource: A source of support.

riot: A violent public disturbance by a group of people.

stress: Something that causes strong feelings of worry.

threat: Someone or something that could cause harm.

violence: The use of force to hurt, harm, or destroy.

INDEX

A
administrator, 39
ally, 33, 36

B
body parts, 8, 9, 12, 15, 18

C
counselor, 24, 30
cyberbullying, 26

D
depression, 32

E
equal rights, 7, 21, 24, 43
experiences, 6, 22

F
females, 8, 9, 14, 15, 19

G
gender, 6, 11, 12, 15
    expression, 12, 14, 15, 18
    relationship to sex, 8–9
gender identities, 7, 11, 12, 14

H
harassment, 21, 25, 40
health, 9
health care, 21, 22, 30
homelessness, 30
hormones, 15
housing, discrimination in, 21, 22
human rights, 19

I
identity, 6, 9, 10, 12, 15, 16, 18, 21, 26, 40, 42
    gender, 7, 11, 12, 14, 25, 38, 42
    sexual, 7, 11, 19, 25

J
jobs, discrimination in, 21, 22

L
laws, 19, 20, 22, 24
lesbian, 7, 10, 11, 16

M
majorities, 7
males, 8, 9, 14, 15, 19
marriage, 22
mental health, 32–33
minorities, 7, 11, 30
    protecting, 18–19

O
operations, 9, 15

P
prejudices, 37, 43
Pride month, 43
pronouns, 14, 25, 28, 36

R
resources, 27
respect, 7, 37, 41

S
same-sex couples, 20, 21, 44
school, 4, 16, 22, 24–25, 27, 28, 30, 34, 38, 39, 44
    rules, 37, 39
sex, relationship with gender, 7, 8–9, 11
sexuality, 6, 11, 16, 43
sexual orientation, 10, 11, 12
slurs, 36
social media, 16, 26, 40
Stonewall riots, 43
stress, 30, 32, 41
suicide, 32

T
transitioning, 14–15

V
violence, 21